Carole Gerber

Leaf Jumpers

Illustrated by Leslie Evans

Charlesbridge

Published by Charlesbridge
85 Main Street
Watertown, MA 02472
(617) 926-0329
www.charlesbridge.com

Library of Congress Cataloging-in-Publication Data
Gerber, Carole.
   Leaf jumpers / Carole Gerber ; illustrated by Leslie Evans.
      p. cm.
Summary: Illustrations and rhyming text describe different leaves
and the trees from which they fall.
   ISBN-13: 978-1-57091-497-3; ISBN-10: 1-57091-497-4 (reinforced for library use)
   ISBN-13: 978-1-57091-498-0; ISBN-10: 1-57091-498-2 (softcover)
   1. Leaves—Juvenile literature. 2. Trees—Juvenile literature.
[1. Leaves. 2. Trees.] I. Evans, Leslie, 1953- ill. II. Title.
QK649.G36 2004
575.5'7—dc22   2003015846

Printed in Korea
(hc) 10 9 8 7 6 5 4
(sc) 10 9 8 7 6 5 4

Illustrations made from linoleum block prints and watercolors on Arches paper
Display type and text type set in Clearface
Color separated, printed, and bound by Sung In Printing, Korea
Production supervision by Brian G. Walker and Linda Jackson
Designed by Susan Mallory Sherman

In memory of my sister Barbara Brockmeier, who loved
to rake leaves   —C. G.

For Amelia and Charlie and the many happy autumn days
                                                  —L. E.

We watch a soft wind shake the trees.
It lifts the leaves and sets them free.

Released, they flutter through the air,
drifting downward gracefully.

We run to catch the falling leaves.

We smell their smells and touch their veins.

Bright jewels from the crowns of trees . . .

We trace their shapes. We say their names.

Red maple's broad and pointed leaves
flame bright and vivid as a match.

The sugar maple's leaves are orange,
like pumpkins in a pumpkin patch.

Stubby fingers, brown as dirt,
reach from the slender white oak leaf.

The basswood's glowing yellow leaves
are shaped like hearts with little teeth.

The birch leaf, oval as an egg,
falls sunny-side upon the ground.

Willow leaves turn yellow-green
and hang from limbs that all
curve down.

The ginkgo's wavy golden leaf
is shaped just like a little fan.

The broad leaf of the sycamore
is yellow with a coat of tan.

We toss the bright leaves in the air:
oranges, yellows, golds, and reds.
We dance together as they fall.
Leaf hats settle on our heads.

We clap with joy.

We love the leaves!

We rake a glowing, golden heap.

Then, holding hands, we jump into
a pile of colors, three feet deep.

Ginkgo

White Oak

Sycamore

Leaves that turn
bright colors in the autumn were green
during the spring and summer. During
those seasons, the green leaves make food
for the tree from water, air, and sunshine.
The "tree food" made in the leaves is a
kind of sugar that keeps
the leaves alive and
helps the tree to grow.

Basswood

In the fall, the weather turns
colder. There is not enough sunshine
and rain for the leaves to make food for
the tree. Their job is done, and the tree stops
growing. It has no further use for its leaves, so
they begin to die.

Sugar Maple

Then, something beautiful happens—the
leaves change colors! Out come the yellow and
orange hues that, during spring and summer, were
covered by shades of green. Other changes in the leaves
make the red and brown colors come out, too. The leaves
containing the most stored food turn the brightest
colors before they fall to the ground.

Willow

Red Maple

Birch